A Time To Rhyme

Maurine Wilder

Maurine Wilder

DEDICATION

Dedicated to those whose lives have touched mine; therefore, allowing me the opportunity to share with others my faith, humor, joys and sorrows.

CONTENTS

Early Writings

FASHIONS

Many, many years ago
A hundred years or more,
The women wore dresses
While standing by the shore.

They had long sleeves
And quite full skirts.
The men in breeches
And stiff-collared shirts.

They thought that it was modern then,
And I guess maybe it was, too;
But I don't think I'd like to wear them.
I don't think you would. Would you?

(Age 12)

THE TEEN YEARS

The 'teen years', it seems to me,
Are the happiest years of your life.
They're full of anger, toils, and snares,
Also happiness, love, and strife.

To me, they're passing all too fast;
I do wish they'd linger on.
I don't know how, but maybe it's true:
"The best years are yet to come."

(Age 16)

MOTHER'S DAY

On this, your day,
Just once in a year,
I'm proud I can say
To you, my dear,
I love you, Mother,
With all my heart.
There'll never be another,
And never will we part.

And here, dear Mother,
Is my gift to you.
It cost no more
Than a dollar or two.
But my heart's in it,
And ever will be.
Take it, enjoy it,
In remembrance of me.

(Age 17)

THANKSGIVING

Thanksgiving day is almost here,
And all the world is filled with cheer.

We just got a letter from Uncle Fred.
"We'll be there soon" is what it said.

The telephone rang, and rang, and rang.
"We're coming, too!" cousin Ned sang.

The telegraph boy just arrived at the door.
Grandma and Grandpa will be here at four.

Let's bow our heads in grateful praise,
And unto the Lord our voices raise.

For friends, for food, for loved ones dear,
We give our thanks again this year.

(Age 12)

5

CHRISTMAS

When Christmas time comes every year
And snow is on the ground,
I like to hear the sleigh bells ring,
And the children's happy sound.

When we went shopping yesterday,
We had a lot of fun!
I got my baby brother
A little top that spun.

I got my Mother a doo-dad shelf,
And sister a great big ball.
And Daddy a tie and pretty white shirt.
I spent ten dollars in all!

When comes the time of Christmas Eve,
We plan to pop some corn;
And sing some Christmas carols
To remind us when Christ was born.

I'd like to hear the story again
How Jesus was born in the hay;
How His mother Mary took care of Him
When in the manger He lay.

And when this Christmas time has passed,
And we've welcomed in the new year,
I'll hope we have a lot of fun
When Christmas comes next year!

(Age 12)

CLOSE OF THE DAY

Dusk is creeping over the city.
The sun is waving good-bye.
Darkness will be here before we know it;
Moon and stars will be floating on high.

People are leaving their jobs, their work;
Some look so weary and worn.
This night to them will mean blessed rest;
But it all will end with the birth of the morn.

~~~~~

The sun is gone completely now;
And sure enough, there are the stars.
The moon is just a sliver of light;
The beautiful peace of the night is ours.
Another day of our life is gone, gone, gone.
But in a short length of time, tomorrow will dawn.

(Age 16)

POETIC PROBLEMS

I'm trying to write a poem,
But nothing seems to rhyme.
The words seem to fit perfectly
'Til I get to the end of the line.

Now, see! I've done it again!
'Rhyme' and 'line' don't sound the same.
The right words just can't be found.
My efforts are all in vain.

'Vain' and 'same'. Isn't that silly?
They don't sound at all alike.
One ends in 'N', the other 'M'.
I'd like to quit. I think I might!

This is the close. The very end.
I've failed so many times.
But read this verse again, you'll see
A miracle! It rhymes!

(Age 17)

THE HANDS OF GOD

It may be only a towering tree,
Or a rose that is withering and small;
Sometimes just a weed on a barren plain,
But the hands of God made it all.

It may be only a blade of grass,
Or a mountain extremely tall;
Just a cornfield on a run-down farm,
But the hands of God made it all.

It may be only a crumbling leaf,
Or a star that might tumble and fall;
A mansion in heaven that's waiting for me,
And the hands of God made it all!

(Age 16)

9

Humor

&

Nonsense

HOUSEWORK VERSUS SHOPPING

Dishes, dishes, dishes;
Is that job ever done?
Laundry, laundry, laundry;
Is that job ever fun?
Cooking, cooking, cooking;
It sure keeps me on the run.
Shopping, shopping, shopping;
Now that's what I call fun!

MY BEST FRIEND

Chocolate is my best friend!
But this is what I think:
Perhaps I ate too much of it ~
For Chocolate made my clothes shrink!

DIET

Dieting is not my passion,
And, yes, I've binged and binged.
So now I find that I've become
Proportionately challenged!

THE TRIALS AND TRIBULATIONS OF SO MANY BIRTHDAYS

"The best is yet to come", we often hear people say.
For you, the wait is over and this is your lucky day!

Roses are red and violets are blue.
You think others are old? Well, now you are, too!

Do you use 'readers', worn by the masses?
Soon you will need bifocal glasses.

No longer walking steadily, or climbing stairs with grace?
Perhaps a walker or a cane could put a smile on your face.

Having trouble hearing what other people say?
Hearing aids with batteries will brighten up your day.

Are you missing a few teeth? Lower ones and uppers?
Soon you'll need false ones to enjoy your daily suppers.

Is kneeling a problem because of your knees?
Replacements are available for exorbitant fees.

Can't recall words and names? Can't find all you've got?
Yes, the memory's slipping ~~ and sharp you now are not!

Innards noisily growling, producing odors with tunes?
Stop feasting on the good stuff ~~ and then bring on the prunes.

Eating too much, as usual, and a bellyache often comes?
Give up all the tasty things, and gobble down the Tums.

When your special day is over, and all is said and done,
Just enjoy the memories of your birthday and its fun!

14

HOT FLASHES

Hot flashes are filled with emotion,
And incredible amounts of heat.
My forehead gets moist, my ears turn pink,
And my face is as red as a beet.

Quick! Where's my fan? I need it right now!
Oh, where have I laid it? Oh, where?
By the phone? The sink? The ironing board?
On the desk? The table? Or by my chair?

I'm desperate! Dripping! Really upset!
Then I see it! Only a few steps away!
I grab it, fan fast, and I wonder:
How many more will I have yet today?

This, too, will pass, so I've been told,
By ladies much older than me.
I really look forward to that time
For much happier I'm sure I will be.

DESSERTS

Desserts are so delicious!
They really hit the spot!
However, trim and slender
Is what I now am NOT!

YIKES! I HAVE NO MORE MONEY!

Yikes! I have no more money!
I have no more money to spend.
I had some, I recall,
Till I shopped at the mall.
Now I am at my wit's end.

When can I get some more money,
Get some without any fuss?
That's no problem, I say,
Because most any day,
I'll get my share of "stimulus"!

Will I have to repay it
Some day when I'm 'over the hill'?
No, it's totally free,
With no charge to me.
My grandkids will pay the bill!

TO THE NEW MOTHER

If washing diapers makes you gag,
And plastic poo-poo's not your bag,
Then here's the very latest "scoop":
Let your husband wash the poop!

TO SOMEONE "SITTING-NOT-TOO-MUCH"

A 'little bird' came to visit,
And clued me in on you.
He said your current problem
Wasn't considered 'just the flu'.

He said quite often he has seen
You wearing many frowns,
Because the 'standing up' was great;
But oh! Those 'sitting downs'!

So as I offer this advice,
Don't 'wrinkle up your nose'.
When sitting's not a pleasure,
Try hanging by your toes!

ODE TO A MOTHER'S EARS

The yells, the squeals, the bangs, the booms,
That are coming forth from all our rooms,
Are something of which I am aware
But don't control. Why do I care?

Because those sounds are louder than
A whistling train or lumbering van.
None compare with all the noise
That emanates from my small boys!

THE CURE

My motivator's broken.
All ambition has left me.
Tempted I am to sit all day,
And a 'couch potato' be.

But "laziness" is fattening,
I'm sure somewhere I've read.
And "busy hands are happy hands",
I've often heard it said.

So now I'm feeling guilty
About how my time is spent.
I'll concentrate and try to find
Where my "get-up-and-go" went.

There must be something helpful,
Some where to find a cure.
I know! I'll eat some chocolate!
Then I'll be energized for sure!

CHOCOLATE

Chocolate! Chocolate! Chocolate!
It can really hit the spot
Whenever you are feeling good,
But especially when you're NOT!

PILLS

In your opinion,
Big pills sure stink,
And stick in your throat
Quick as a wink.

But I've a solution
That I am sure will
Make it really easy
To swallow a pill.

Chew up a peach slice
That's slimy and slick;
Then pop in that pill
And swallow real quick.

In no time at all,
It will go quickly down.
Then you'll wear a smile
Instead of a frown.

Well, I'm very sure
You'll see what I mean.
Now, ain't this idea
Just "peachy keen"?

40TH BIRTHDAY

It's been said that 'forty is sporty',
And seemingly not very old;
That life looks rosy before you.
At least that's what you've been told.

But spoken by one who has 'been there',
You're well on your way to the 'hill',
Where you'll be known as a 'senior'
With many prescriptions to fill.

So now is the time to enjoy life,
To travel, to laugh, and to play;
To treasure your friends and family
Who celebrate with you today.

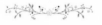

HAPPY 50TH BIRTHDAY

It must sadden you to notice
That this magazine is old.

The pictures are old fashioned;
The news in it is cold.

The pages are quite wrinkled.
The colors are faded, too.

Guess what I just noticed ~
It looks a lot like you!

ARTHUR

When Arthur comes to visit,
My life grows rather dim.
And though he comes quite often,
I'm still not used to him.

Does he come on sunny days?
The ones that seem so bright?
Oh, no! He always picks a time
When humidity's a fright!

Still, I cannot turn him out,
For he's sharp as a tack;
And aspirin seems the only thing
To turn old Arthur back.

Sometimes he drives me to my chair,
And makes me walk with canes.
For 'Arthur' is the name I've given
My arthritis pains.

A NASTY COLD

My cold is quite obnoxious!
It makes me cough and sputter.
I'll sure be glad when it is gone,
So 'bad words' I don't mutter.

WHEN SUPPORT IS NEEDED
(Included was a girdle supporter)

If support's what you need
On a day like today,
Then I'd like to lend
Some help... if I may.

A shoulder to cry on
Won't help you at all;
For if you leaned on me,
We both might fall!

At a time like this,
A good friend I should be;
But encouraging words
Are eluding me.

You'll find here enclosed
Help of a different sort.
It's guaranteed to give
The best kind of support!

YES, I AM BLIND, BUT ~~

Yes I am blind; but I can see
You're standing way too close to me!
How do I know? What gave you away?
You failed to use deodorant today!

A ZIPPER 'OOPS'

"Your zipper is open,"
A friend told me one day.
So now I check it quite often
Throughout the day.

I must 'zipper up',
So nothing will show.
And I can hold my head high
Wherever I go.

A HUNTER'S SUCCESS

I got it! Yes, I really did!
And I am very glad
That feisty little pig is mine.
And, man! What fun I had!

I'm going to have it mounted
And hang it up to show;
Because I'm very, very sure
The whole world wants to know!

MY WISH FOR YOU

"I wish you joy and happiness,
And love that knows no bounds.

I wish you lots of chocolate,
And hope it adds no pounds!"

MOVIE STARS

Josh played a 'major' role
In the movie of my life.
His part was the imperfect husband;
I 'starred' as the imperfect wife!

LOTS OF BIRTHDAYS

I've had so many birthdays,
So this is what I think:
Perhaps I've had so many
That soon I'll start to stink!

ASHES TO ASHES

Ashes to ashes,
Dust to dust.
I'll die some day,
When God says I must.

'APE' LIMERICK

There was a big fat ape
Who tried to wear a cape.

She twisted and twirled
Until it unfurled,

And strangled her neck at the nape!

FAT CAT

A couple once had a big spat
Over who would feed their cat.

"I'll do it", said he.
"I will, too," said she.

And quickly the cat became fat!

A HUNTER'S LIMERICK

A hunter I know – Tom's his name ~
Needs a lesson on how to shoot game.

More often than not
He misses his shot,

And blows all his chances for fame.

CONTROL

As an older lady, I now find
My bladder's quite 'unruly'.
Sometimes it acts without warning,
Which embarrasses 'yours truly'.

EATHEL'S LIMERICK

There was a lady who bumped her toe.
And it received a mighty blow.

"It was almost lethal"
Said little Eathel.

Now she'll watch wherever she might go!

OLDER SKIN

Is my skin still smooth and soft?
Does it feel like velvet? NOPE!
It has become wrinkles and ridges.
Will it improve? I only can hope!

AN OLD LADY'S LAMENT

When I was young ~
I ran out of time before I ran out of energy.

Now that I'm old ~
I run out of energy before I run out of time!

BALLOON LIMERICK

I tried to blow up a balloon,
And swelled up like a cocoon.

I soon lost the race
When it blew up in my face.

Friends said I looked like a baboon!

WAYNE THE TRIVIA BUFF

*Lend an ear, and I'll wager you'll find
That Wayne has a very trivial mind!*

*It delights him no end to set friends ajar
With tidbits of knowledge from both near and
far.*

*Many the time we've heard him report
Items of news with little import.*

*Like what kind of soup has little pizzazz,
And how many Z's in razzamatazz.*

*Or where in the world was the first gold panned,
And who once directed the world's largest band.*

*True, he helps keep conversations quite merry;
But as to the facts, you better be wary!*

*Others like him are impossible to find,
So thankful are we that he's one of a kind!*

Red Hat Ladies

RAZZLE DAZZLE RED HAT CHEER

We're the Razzle Dazzle Red Hats!
We're out to have some fun!

We're the Razzle Dazzle Red Hats!
We're often on the run!

We wear Red Hats above our nose
And purple clothes down to our toes.

Razzle Dazzle Red Hats!
YEAH!

"DON'T YOU THINK I LOOK SPIFFY?"
(Tune: Rudolph the Red Nosed Reindeer)

Don't you think I look real pretty
In my hat and purple clothes?
Don't you think that I look spiffy
With jewelry from my head to toes?
All of the other ladies
Are just as gorgeous as me!
No one could ever argue,
For our beauty's plain to see.

31

RED HAT SOCIETY

Some think I look old.
Some think I look fat.
Some think I look silly
In my fancy red hat.

Some think I am crazy!
Some might even profess
I'm just an old biddy
In a bright purple dress.

Who cares what they think!
For what do they know?
I'm sure I look gorgeous
From head to toe.

All of my friends
Think just like me,
Because we belong to
The "Red Hat Society"!

RAZZLE DAZZLE RED HAT HISTORY

The date was August, Two Thousand Four,
When first we gathered, and our red hats we wore.

Razzle Dazzle Red Hats became our name.
Having fun with friends became our game.

Some objected to a red hat on their head;
But 'rules are rules', and their worries fled.

And the purples we were told to wear?
Some thought it better than going bare!

For eight years we've worn our purple and red,
And ignored the remarks some 'outsiders' said.

Decked out in boas, bracelets, and rings,
We knew we looked great for all our outings!

In our royal colors, and with our heads held high,
We rode in parades, waving like Princess Di.

We each gave our self a 'royal' name,
Describing ourselves ~~ with no two the same.

Whether Dame, or Countess, or Princess, or such,
Each name was special and meant very much.

The third Tuesday each month we gathered to eat,
Then drove to fun places; did tours on our feet.

We sang birthday songs, with a 'kazoo's' loud trill,
Which gave 'birthday ladies' an embarrassing thrill!

We partied at Christmas, then broke out in song
With familiar tunes, funny words, in voices so strong.

We dined, and feasted, and ate and ate,
Then added desserts, and promptly gained weight.

We traveled in boldness, without any fear,
Laughing and singing, and reciting our 'cheer'.

Drivers a plenty? Can't say that was true;
But we always found room for me and for you.

In our prettiest clothes, we drove many miles
To watch "Menopause", which brought giggles and
smiles.

We entertained at Prime Time lunch,
Where they all considered us a lively bunch!

We saw ladies stitch purses, and monogram hats.
We watched men construct windows, and baseball bats.

We all used our Red Hat fans with grace,
Which made us more comfy ~~ especially our face.

At a TV station we were welcomed with joy
By Tricia who's pretty, and Gordy who's coy.

On Lake Michigan, we sailed in a yacht.
Then at a casino, we won big ~~ NOT!

We watched workers make paper from a watery mess.
And how can that happen? We can only guess!

We ate, and we ate, and we ate even more,
Indulged in pies, cakes, goodies, and more!

The Queen gave us brushes. For our hair? Oh no!
They were for our 'belly buttons' that we never show!

34

We shopped till we dropped! Then shopped some more!
We even went shopping in a Red Hat store.

We trotted here, and we trotted there.
We even trotted to a Courthouse Square.

We went to a bakery. With the Amish had lunch.
Made bracelets with beads. Saw cigars ~~ quite a
bunch!

We visited an artist; rode on two boats;
Saw alpacas and llamas feeling their oats.

We went to museums of clothes, circus, and glass.
Emma showed us her eggs of brilliance and class.

We ate candy at factories, so now we're not 'lean'.
Visited a Police Post. We saw a knitting machine.

We saw cows at a dairy, and the making of cheese,
Watched Crete do her spinning ~~ without any fees.

We observed a potter, even shopped in his store;
Went on a hayride, bought pumpkins and more.

What would we take for all the good times we had?
Nothing at all, because our hearts were made glad.

The last eight years have simply flown
Since we became a group of our own.

With never a squabble and seldom a fuss,
Nothing important ever bothered us.

Forever we'll miss the two who've passed on:
Our sweet Gen Scheffer and kind Linda Braun.

But time changes people. And time changes things.
Yes, it is evident the changes time brings.

As we look to the future, we'll still keep in touch,
For Red Hatters are special ~ we care and love much.

Today may our time together be happy ~~ not sad,
For our years together have been more 'good' than
'bad'.

This was written by the Queen who likes rhyme. You know
~ the one who hopes you've had a grand time!

"RED HAT GIRLS"
(Tune: Jingle Bells)

Red Hat girls, Red Hat girls,
Today let's have some fun!
Oh what joy it is to eat
In this gymnasium!
Red Hat girls, Red Hat girls,
We'll gain a pound or two.
But if you still will be my friend,
I'll be one back to you.

Odds & Ends

MESSAGE FROM A FROG

__F__orever I will strive to
__R__ely both night and day
__O__n the One I can trust, the
__G__od who guides my way.
Forever Rely On God

THANK YOU TO A FRIEND

Thoughtful friends are a blessing
In life that we would not trade.
You are listed among those
Whose kindness cannot be repaid.

Please be assured that your gift
Of much use for years will be.
The thankfulness in my heart
Will forever be in my memory.

THE LIAR

She fabricates, exaggerates,
She tells 'tall takes' and lies.
She grossly overstates the facts,
And thus the truth defies.

HOMEMADE IS BEST
(Tune: Home on the Range)

Oh, give me a scrap,
Send the kids for a nap,
And I'll make something homemade each time.

For I seldom feel blue,
If I make something new,
And I might even save a dime.

Chorus:
Homemade is best!
It's great when I make things from 'scratch',
Such as sewing a quilt, canning green beans, or
Baking cookies by the batch!

I AM SO BLESSED

I am so blessed.
God has saved me.

I am so blessed.
He has graced me
With his love
That truly fills me.

I am so blessed!

MY CHRISTMAS STOCKING

This stocking may look empty,
But in truth there's much inside.
It's bulging with some history
That with you I'll now confide.

The fabric once was part of
A gown your grandma wore.
In fact, the day she married,
It grandly swept the floor.

Her dress has been refashioned.
The stitching is brand new.
This very fine creation's now
A keep-sake ~~ just for you!

FRIENDSHIP

Sharing my burden
With you, dear friend,
Makes carrying it
So much lighter.

Knowing you love
And care for me
Makes my whole day
Very much brighter!

A SUMMER CRUISE

Shout it from the rooftops!
Tell every one the news!
Four young and crazy women
Are going on a cruise.

With permission from the hubbies,
Plus passes from their zoos!
And with blessing from their Pastor,
They're ready for the cruise.

They have packed their clothing.
They have packed their shoes.
They have packed their make-up.
All are needed on a cruise.

With passports in their purses,
And pills so they won't lose
Their recent dinners overboard!
They're set to start their cruise.

They plan to snap some pictures.
No time to take a snooze!
They'll do some serious sunning
While sailing on that cruise.

They know the time will pass
More quickly than they choose.
Too soon the Captain will announce
The ending of their cruise.

They'll re-pack their belongings
And try to thwart the blues.
Those four tired sunburned women
Returning from their cruise.

The hugs and smiles they'll share
Will be sufficient clues
That they will forever treasure
The memories of their cruise.

CRUISE ENDING

It's all over but the shouting.
Almost time to say goodbye.
The cruise was really wonderful.
Oh! How the days did fly!

Time may fade the memories
Of our sailing on the sea;
Time can't touch this memory:
"Friends forever we will be."

REFLECTIONS

Reflecting on the year just past,
Many memories come to mind.
Some are pleasant, bringing joy,
Others are of a different kind.

There were times of brilliant sunshine
When the heart so happy was;
When a carefree day brought laughter
To cheer us, as it always does.

There were seasons of great sadness
When grief rained darkness on the soul;
Creating tears that flowed so freely.
Yes, the loss of someone takes its toll.

When it rained, the Lord held closely
The ones who suffered much that day.
Until the sunshine did return,
Lifting their spirits along the way.

Rain and sunshine are parts of life
That God uses often to help show
That He's still in charge and loves us.
Reflecting helps our faith to grow.

ANOTHER BIRTHDAY!

As you're adding one more birthday,
And you see the number's grown,
It might make you stop and wonder
Where those many years have flown.

Those birthdays come along so fast;
But for each one, no doubt you're glad
That your time on earth continued,
And many precious times you've had.

As you walk into tomorrow
And the future's open door,
May your life be filled with pleasure
And your birthdays many more!

COLLEGE DAYS

I'm 'rushing' but getting no where.
In fact, I'm staying in one place.
Because I'm a college Freshman,
It's a sorority I chase!

RELATIONSHIPS

If what we say and what we do
Builds walls or bridges between me and you,
Then we must always do and say
The kindest thing in a pleasant way.

Harsh and cruel words burn like fire
And tend to build walls higher and higher
Until relationships that once were great
Suffer much damage ~~ and then its too late.

How much better the world would be
If we could all learn that love is the key
To building strong bridges that will bear
The weight of relationships, precious and rare.

So let's be gentle, and let's be kind
To one another; and we will find
That everything we say and do
Will build a bridge between me and you.

CHRISTMAS GIFT

It doesn't seem like Christmas,
With no snow on the ground.
And yet the Christmas spirit
Deep in our hearts is found.

We're thankful for this time of year
That gives the chance to share
With very special people
For whom we really care.

Today, we surely hope this gift
Will give you special reason
To purchase something very nice.
Enjoy this Christmas season!

TRANSITION

Transition's not always easy,
And change often causes some pain;
But as time passes and we look back,
We discover no loss ~~ just gain.

PAST-DUE BABY

Roses are red,
Violets are blue
We're getting tired
Waiting on you!

The nurses are ready,
The doctor's 'on-call'.
Husband's impatient
So get on the ball!

Time to deliver
A lass or a lad
To make you and hubby
A Mom and a Dad.

As long as we must,
We'll sit by the phone
To get all the news
From "Maternity Zone".

Of course, you know
We're rooting for you.
So lots of luck
And best wishes, too!

DINNER GUESTS

So glad we are that you've come,
You, and your lovely wife.
We trust the dinner that's prepared
Won't poison you for life!

The culinary's simple;
But, then, the cook is, too!
Fellowship's what matters;
That's why we invited you.

Now dig right in; enjoy yourself.
Then please destroy this rhyme.
Relax, and make yourselves at home
And come again another time.

THE POWER OF A PEN

A pen carries with it great power
To construct, entertain, and convey.
Words enlighten the minds of readers,
Possibly even guiding their way.

Dream big! Write often! Then share
With those in the world where you live.
The thoughts you write are important.
From your heart, you have much to give.

Use your pen boldly, but wisely,
With those you will chance to meet.
Years later, when you pause to reflect,
You'll find your life has been complete.

THE REASON FOR THE SEASON

"Jesus is the reason for the season',
We've heard some people say.
Perhaps they've learned the meaning
Of that first glad Christmas Day.

Many, many years have passed
Since God's son came to earth,
Offering us the gift of love
That resulted from His birth.

In love God sent His only son
To save us from our sin.
In love He beckons tenderly
To change the lives of men.

As we respond, He fills us with
A love we're asked to share;
To make the world a better place,
As each other's burdens we bear.

Today we know without a doubt
Why Jesus came from above;
It was to show us, still today,
"The reason for the season is love."

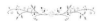

ROAD TO SOMEWHERE

Walk with me, if you dare,
And walk a Road to Somewhere.

We'll 'go it' together.
Who knows where it leads!
For long ago, fate
Took a handful of seeds
And planted the way.
Let's journey together today.

Can anyone tell what life may hold?
We'll walk together! And we'll walk bold!

Where does life lead us?
Just to an end?
Perhaps much further,
I tell you, my friend.
But we must travel
The road straight and true,
If we want to find something
Out there beyond the blue.

Walk with me. Yes, since you dare,
We'll travel together a Road to Somewhere.

LIFE GOES SO FAST

Life
Goes
So
Fast.

Only yesterday, it seems,
Dad reached down.

To help, teach, and touch me.

But then I grew so fast.

His reaching down
Became reaching over.

Building a bridge.
A bond, more love.

He left yesterday.
So
Fast.
Wet tears remind me,
Assure me. Console me.

The best friend I had was Dad.
Life
Goes
So
Fast.

53

MRS. LINOLN'S 'LIGHT BULB'

Mrs. Lincoln's 'light bulb'
Lights up when she perceives
A wonderful idea for someone
In whom she really believes.

That's when the wheels start turning,
And we all get in the act.
Soon she's sure that her idea
Is really being backed.

When the job's done, the credit goes
To all ~~ and that is fine.
But it was on Mrs. Lincoln
That the light first did shine.

SOME LIKE TO CREATE
(Tune: Back Home Again in Indiana)

Some like to knit, some like to crochet,
They find joy in those things.

Some even like to paint
Pictures bright or faint,
Then watch the smiles they bring.

Some like to sew, some do some writing.
Some may play a happy tune.

When I think about the good things I can create,
Then I thank God for giving life to me.

WILDER MINI REUNION

On Saturday, the third of June
In nineteen-hundred ninety-five,
Wilders from both near and far
In Winamac, Indiana, did arrive.

The purpose of the gathering?
A Mini-Reunion it was called,
First on the agenda was pictures
Of family with hair, and some bald!

The ten of us posed very fast!
It was a MUST, we all agreed;
For if we slowed down much at all,
The mosquitoes on us would feed!

The 'remember whens' began early
And continued throughout the week.
We recalled events in years gone by,
At old memories, we took a peek.

A highlight of the reunion was
A Christmas Together – in June!
Complete with tree, and gifts for all,
The joy won't be forgotten soon.

We talked and we played together,
We worked ~ doing laundry and such.
We all went to church on Sunday,
We laughed ~ and we ate too much.

Too quickly our visit was ended,
And we all went our separate ways;
We each took along in our hearts
Great memories of those special days!

We'll remember our hugs of greeting.
We'll remember the goodbye tears.
We'll remember the time we created.
Precious memories for future years.

Love & Friendship

A GARDEN OF LOVE
"A Wedding Gift"

Good marriages often
Fit like a glove,
When two lives are joined
In friendship and love.

Gloves for the groom
With a gift to buy hoes,
Or maybe a hammer
When shopping at Lowe's.

The delicate gloves
Have hidden inside
A gift to buy flowers
By the beautiful bride.

Treasure each day
From dusk until dawn,
As you walk hand in hand
From this day on.

ON YOUR WEDDING DAY

Hand in hand the two of you
Plan to walk for many years ~~
In times of joy and laughter,
Sometimes sorrow and its tears.

Through it all, your love will grow
If to each other you stay true.
Your inner beauty will be evident
In each other's point of view.

The future now is waiting.
You'll surely find it grand!
May you walk together always
As you hold each other's hand.

ROMANCE

When life brings us change
And some joys have dwindled,
There's nothing better
Than a romance rekindled.

BECAUSE I CARE

When your waters are troubled, I flounder, too.
Because I care.

When you experience depression, I'm down in
the dumps.
Because I care.

When your eyes brim with tears, my own
overflow.
Because I care.

Then again ~~

As you ask of the Lord, He'll hear my cry, too.
Because I care.

As you ascend from the valley, I'll wave from the
mountain.
Because I care.

As your full smile returns, I'll bubble with joy!
Because I care.

MEMORY OF A FRIEND

My friend was special in so many ways.
She gladdened my heart and brightened my days.

We shared silly laughter, bear hugs, and tears.
We shared concern, and some of our fears.

That sharing and caring caused our friendship to
grow.
We trusted each other more than most people
know.

Together we sailed the ocean blue.
Making fun memories. More than a few.

The memory I treasure more than all the rest,
Was the glow on her face whenever God blessed.

When God touched her heart, He made her new,
Then she prayed and shared with all whom she
knew.

She allowed God to use her; she surrendered her
all.
Until today ~~ when God in His heaven did call.

My memories of her are precious, for you see,
Oh, how I loved my Friend!
And how my friend loved me!

62

I TREASURE YOUR FRIENDSHIP

Sometimes love is like osmosis,
As from heart to heart it flows.
Gracing lives with warm emotion,
Creating friendships as it goes.

Knowing you has been a privilege.
Loving you has come easily.
Oh, how much I truly treasure
The friend that you've become to me.

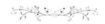

TO MY VALENTINE

My love for you has multiplied
Since Nineteen Fifty-Nine.
So today I want you to know
I'm so glad you're still mine.

Today I love you even more
Than I loved you yesterday.
I'll love you more tomorrow
Than I even do today!

A SPECIAL FRIENDSHIP

You stood by me when I was weak, and when I was weary.
You stood by me when life seemed more than I could bear.
When I needed a touch of love and compassion,
You stood nearby and showed me how much you care.

You stood by me when hope was gone and I was lonesome.
You stood by me when I needed someone with whom to
share.
When I needed the prayers of the true and the faithful,
You stood nearby and assured me you'd stay there.

Some day you may find your life's no longer rosy.
Some day your worries may become more than a few.
When you're seeking someone to give you comfort,
That's when you'll find that I'll be there for you.

Some day you may view the world as quite unfriendly.
Some day you may find that life's lost it's rosy hue.
When you need a hug or someone you can lean on,
That's when I'll be there to pray and stand by you.

Together we can walk life's hills and life's valleys.
Together we can search for the happiest way.
Sharing and caring, our friendship will flourish
And become more precious every day.

As friends, we'll consider the other one special.
As friends, for the other we'll seek only the best.
And by saving a corner of our hearts for each other,
We'll find we are rich ~~ for with friendship we're
blessed.

YOUR LIFE TOUCHED MINE

You question why I care so much,
And shower you with love,
Presenting you with little gifts
And tidbits from God above.

You ask why in your trying time
When life is standing still,
That I would gladly take your place
If it could only be God's will.

The answer is within yourself.
Your life you chose to share.
That's why today I am convinced
A friend like you is rare.

Whenever I reached out my hand,
You walked the second mile.
And when my heart was breaking,
You comforted with a smile.

Months and years, joy and tears.
Such mingled thoughts combine,
Reminding me that I've been blessed
Because your life touched mine.

HAPPY ANNIVERSARY

Hand in hand the two of you
Have walked for many years;
In times of joy and laughter,
Also sorrow and it's tears.

Through it all, your love has grown
As to each other you've stayed true.
Your inner beauty's fairer still
In each other's point of view.

The future still is waiting.
You'll surely find it grand!
May you walk together always
As you hold each other's hand.

NEW FRIEND

There's nothing like a new friend
Knocking at your door;
A friend you'll enjoy forever.
A friend that makes your spirit soar.

WEDDING ANNIVERSARY

The flowers that I boasted
Upon my dress lapel,
Sent me a lovely fragrance
That no one else could smell.

Sure, friends caught the aroma
Of flowers in fresh bloom,
As my lovely red carnations
Brightened up the room.

But they saw only beauty
That corsages can convey,
While I was sensing something
Much more beautiful that day.

You see, the flowers all were tied
With ribbons bright and red;
But they were also bound with love.
"For you alone', the sender said.

So today I actually received
The fragrance of love sincere,
And my heart was warmed again
By the one I hold most dear.

The thoughtful person in my life,
The one I'm proud to claim,
Is the husband that I cherish ~~
The man who changed my name.

A DREAM RIDE FOR BROTHERS
(One alive, one deceased)

Too young my life was ended,
Too quickly fun had fled.
Too soon I journeyed to heaven,
With a dream still in my head.

The dream was me on a Harley,
With you on one by my side.
Together we'd head for Sturgis.
Wow! What a dream of a ride.

Today I'm traveling with you.
Please pause before you start,
And place me in your pocket;
The one closest to your heart.

Let's hit the trail! Have some fun!
We two will make a memory.
It will be so very special, for
It includes both you and me.

And when we return, I'll say with great pride:
"I love you brother. Thanks for the ride!"

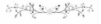

A GIFT OF CASH

With no 'strings attached'
This gift comes to you;
For burgers and fries
Or 'dinner for two'.

For travel expenses,
Some bills that are due,
More than one hundred stamps,
Or something brand new.

Whatever your needs,
Which are more than a few,
Please know when it's gone,
No accounting is due.

The gift comes with love
And it's for all of you.

GOOD FRIENDS

God brought us together for a reason.
Forever and ever?
Or just for a season?
Whatever His motive, whatever His plan,
We'll be good friends
As long as we can.

Personal Touch

MOTHER'S BUTTONS

This pin is special.
Made just for you
From Mother's buttons.
There were only a few.

It's something to keep,
That you'll be proud of.
Wear it with pleasure
And feel Mother's love.

THANK YOU

For the big part that you did play,
Helping me through my 'special' day;
For the best wishes that you did send,
Reminding me that you're my friend;
For what you added to my surprise,
Bringing a smile ~~ or tears to my eyes;
For all these things, I pause to say:
Thanks so much! You made my day!

A TRIBUTE TO OUR FOLKS

From the oldest to the youngest,
From every girl and boy,
From all the grands and great-grands,
We give this gift with joy.

It fills our hearts with pleasure
To know that maybe now
This trusty 'Sears & Roebuck'
More leisure will allow.

For you have surely earned this,
And much more, the truth to tell!
"A job well done", the record reads
"All seven children turned out well."

But now, dear ones, we must turn
To things of great import.
First, go and get the hamper,
Then hold your nose ~~ and sort!

Here are some very, very short
Instructions you must follow.
Go easy with the detergents,
Or in the soapsuds you might wallow!

Don't' wash black and blue together,
And don't mix red with whites;
For if Dad's 'drawers' come out pink,
Who will settle all the fights?

Don't overload, we beg of you,
Unless you're sure you've passed
Your Red Cross swimming lessons,
And can 'back stroke' really fast!

Your washing days aren't over,
You no doubt realize.
But if they're somewhat easier,
We'll be happy with our surprise.

A great amount of happiness
We hope this gift imparts;
For you see, with love it's filled
From deep within our hearts.

A THANK YOU TO MY FRIENDS

In my new home, there sits a chair,
With nary a wrinkle, and free from wear.
Seventeen friends (imagine that!)
Dug into their pockets and filled a hat.

A brand new chair they purchased for me,
With no strings attached. The card said 'free'.
Today a sign to it I will pin:
"Reserved for you, when you drop in!"

Heartfelt thanks are coming your way,
For taking part in my special day!

MY PILLOWCASE DOLL

My Father's Father's mother ~
Mary Wilder was her name,
Once made a pretty pillowcase.
Then to my family it came.

Her very special handi-work
Will be plain for all to see,
For it has now been made into
A 'pillowcase doll' for me.

Real joy is mine to know I have
This precious doll so fair,
That I can hang upon a wall,
Or set in some small chair.

It will always give me pleasure
To own this piece of history;
And it will help me cherish
My great-grandmother's memory.

SYMPATHY

I cannot bear your loss for you,
Nor take away your pain;
But as time passes, you will know
That sunshine always follows rain.

MY FOOTSTOOL

From my childhood I remember,
From my childhood I recall,
Good times, bad times, fun times.
So important were they all.

As I reminisce and wonder,
As my fleeting thoughts go back,
I think of all the special times,
With fun that had no lack.

When sitting at a long, low bar,
It was as a general rule,
I found myself seated on
My very own bar stool.

For eating snacks and all my meals,
For all kinds of kids' play,
I firmly perched upon my stool,
Year after year, day after day.

Now that I'm much, much older,
Now that my childhood's passed,
Today I was presented with
A memory sure to last.

The old stool's been remodeled.
The top is new and neat,
Providing me for many years
A place to prop my feet!

A PRAYER FOR MY FATHER

Dear Lord,

Last week I chanced to meet an old, old friend.
Remember our parting words which were few?
"If we don't meet again, we'll meet in heaven.
And don't forget to bring someone with you."

Those farewell words how they've haunted me,
As they flashed through my mind day and night.
Bring someone with me to heaven, Lord?
I'll pray more earnestly that I might.

You know my efforts in church work, dear Lord.
As to winning souls, though, I've not done my part.
And so my prayer for days has been:
"Lord, lay some soul upon my heart."

The Bible says, "Be still and you will know".
So I've prayed; and I've waited alright.
Just when I thought my prayers you ignored,
Today the answer came like a light.

Thank you, Jesus, for answering my prayer,
And giving me the name of that soul.
The 'someone' you want me to bring
When I arrive in heaven, and reach my goal.

A still small voice very clearly said:
"Maurine, your father's not heaven bound.
You try to win him before it's too late;
Or his feet won't touch on heaven's ground."

"But the person you've asked me to bring,
The 'someone' you laid on my soul,
That man, my father, lives miles away;
And Satan has him under firm control."

Since I can't talk to him personally, God,
It's plain that all I can do is pray.
I'm praying now that You'll speak to his heart,
And that he'll accept Your salvation today.

Help him to have the courage right now
To take the step that he's never dared.
Help him to understand fully, Lord,
That You love him and always have cared.

Remind him, Jesus, that You're calling still,
That You've never given him up for lost.
Help him this moment to say "Yes, Jesus,
I'm Yours from now on ~~ no matter the cost."

Help him to pray: "Forgive me please, God,
For all my sins ~~ and make me like new.
Help me to have the faith to believe
That you'll accept me because I've asked You."

Father in heaven, when he's prayed like that,
Then Maurine's father will let you take hold.
May he claim heaven to be his new goal,
As you welcome him into Your fold.

And when he feels the relief and joy
That belonging to You can bring,
He'll understand why Maurine and her friend,
And the angels in heaven can sing.

When you've answered this prayer, Lord,
You'll be answering my prayer, too.
And then I can shout to heaven above:
"Lord, I've brought my 'someone' to You."

A MOST UNUSUAL CAKE

The gift was a most unusual cake,
Prepared by the hands of Maurine.
It carried an important message
From someone now unseen.

The 'special dark' Pillsbury cake mix,
And, yes, the 'fudge frosting', too,
Were purchased by Joe, Blessed by God,
And then baked for his favorite few.

You'll notice one piece is missing,
Reserved for Joe's 'older friend'.
The ingredients were a gift to her
In a basket she quickly opened.

Most probably Joe is watching
And seeing a smile on each face.
He's sending a 'chocolate message'
With love from his heavenly place.

MY MOTHER

"Most wonderful Mother in the world:"
I say that with nary a doubt.
And you are sure to agree with me,
After I tell you all about
My Mother.

To her, with problems too great for me,
As a child I always could come.
Her tender ear listened, and then I
Always received encouragement from
My Mother.

Though bills were long, the money short,
She still was full of love.
That's one reason I maintain
No one could ever rise above
My Mother.

As a teen, I scoffed at her ways.
"You're old fashioned" was my reply.
How useless today my life would be
If I had missed the training by
My Mother.

The inner beauty she portrayed
So seldom in this world is found.
I guess that's why you'll always see
So many friends gathered around
My Mother.

"Most wonderful woman I have met!"
All who have known her repeat.
And if you're among the lucky ones,
Some day you may get to meet
My Mother.

FIRST CHRISTMAS
WITHOUT A LOVED ONE

During this Christmas season
As your family gathers near,
We remember someone's missing,
A special person you held dear.

May it help to know you're thought of
In a kind and loving way.
We wish you joy and happiness
That will brighten every day.

We hope the Christ of Christmas
Will bring your heart much cheer,
Giving you strength and comfort
As you begin a brand new year.

MY MOTHER-IN-LAW

My heart was full of fear,
Such jitters you never saw
When I was first introduced
To my Mother-in-law!

For jokes we've always heard
Of Mothers whose sons called "ma".
Boy! Was I surprised when
I met my Mother-in-law!

Sincerity gleamed from her eyes,
And pride was set in her jaw;
And only love came from the heart
Of my Mother-in-law.

A better cook you'll never find,
From cookies, to ham, to slaw.
And no one was more full of fun
Than my Mother-in-law!

Two fine daughters and five big sons,
She raised them all from the raw.
And then I plucked the very best
From my Mother-in-law!

How proud I am that I can claim
The woman with nary a flaw.
Yes, that's my husband's Mother,
My wonderful Mother-in-law.

CONGRATULATIONS!

The honor you received today
Is well deserved; no doubt;
For you are known as a hard worker,
And highly thought about.

You always seem to place the needs
Of others before your own.
So now it's time for you to reap
The seeds of joy that you have sown.

Your friends have gathered here today
From North, South, East and West,
To give us all a chance to say:
Well done! You're one of the best!

CAN'T SEE! CAN'T SEE!

It's plain to see
That I <u>can't</u> see
Nearly as well as <u>you</u> can.
So if you'll help me,
I'll gladly thank thee.
Now don't you think that's a good plan?!

SECRET SISTER

My home is full of goodies
Of a very special kind;
Gifted by a special friend,
The best I'll ever find.

Known only as 'Secret Sister',
She's gone the 'second mile';
Presenting me with special gifts;
The kind that brings a smile.

Her thoughtfulness and kindness
Have given me much pleasure,
And the love that she has shared
Forever will be a treasure.

TO BUD GOBLE

There is a tickle in my nose
That I really would like to take out;
But if I do, the blood will flow,
Making a mess around and about.

Then off we'd go to the hospital ER
For more blood and platelets, you see.
So I'll keep my fingers out of my nose,
To protect my body from 'ME'!

THE BACKWARD ANGEL
(Poem accompanied a pin, the back of an angel)

I'm a very special angel,
As you can clearly see.
No one can see my face;
Only the back of me.

I'm a friend of Jesus,
Guarding your precious heart;
Praying that you and He
Will never grow apart.

Take me with you often,
A symbol of God's love.
Share that love with others.
He'll smile from up above.

GENEROUS GESTURE

Your generous gesture touched my heart,
And brought to my life great cheer.
I'll treasure it always because it came
From someone so precious and dear.

A CHRISTMAS GIFT

This is a most unusual gift for you.
It's 'one of a kind', you see.
It's pattern goes back to days of yore,
And it's special to you from me.

You'll find it's 'tatted', a very old art
That few people know how to do.
I'm blessed with a friend who does it,
And I had her create it just for you.

It's beauty will attract much attention;
It's story and it's history will, too.
Enjoy it for years, and display it with pride.
It comes with love ~~ from me to you.

THE MEMORY TREE

Spring is here ~~ and gardens will grow
When someone takes the time to sow.

From seeds, to sprouts, to blossoms bright,
It takes many hours, both daytime and night.

"Gardens of Music" are quite the same;
And we feel you've sown in Jesus' name.

You've worked and toiled with all our needs
Some are full-blossomed, but mostly we're
weeds.

So in your real garden, we want to take part,
Because you've encouraged each song of our
heart.

And so it is with much love that we
Present you both with this 'Memory Tree'.

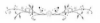

YOU ARE MY UNCLE

(May be sung to the tune of: You are My Sunshine)

You are my Uncle,
My special Uncle.
I'm very lucky
To be your Niece.
Your love abounding
Brings so much pleasure.
You give me joy that does not cease.

Yes, you're my Uncle,
A 'kindly' Uncle.
It's such a privilege
To know your smile.
Though miles and distance
Do separate us,
It's nice to visit once in a while.

My caring Uncle,
Unselfish Uncle,
Your qualities are
More than a few.
Because I saw your
Unselfish nature,
I've learned so very much from you.

You're my dear Uncle,
A precious Uncle.
I'll never, ever,
Forget your ways.
All the good deeds that
You've done for others
Will be remembered all my days.

APPRECIATION

Faithful workers, we appreciate you.
Able workers, we appreciate you.
We take this
Time to thank you
For everything you do.
Trusted workers, we appreciate you.

Loyal workers, we appreciate you.
Tireless workers, we appreciate you.
We thank you.
We praise you.
We owe so very much to you
Unpaid workers, we appreciate you.

WASHINGTON D.C. BUS TRIP

Roses are red, violets are blue;
This is our first trip, and we're glad to meet you!

The roadsides are green, the bus tires are black.
We are the Wilders from small Winamac.

Some poppies are orange, some barns are bright red
Our fearless leaders are named Jim and Ed.

The sun is bright yellow; the sky is so blue.
We stop often for food ~~ and potty breaks, too!

Hyacinths are purple, most dirt is quite brown.
We're heading to D.C., with nary a frown.

Men's suits are navy. Baby pigs are pink.
Our trip will be over, quick as a wink.

Sunsets are peachy; Winter snow is white.
Boy! Won't our beds feel good tonight?!

The ocean is aqua; battle ships are gray.
This poem is silly. What do YOU say?

WASHINGTON D.C. LIMERICKS

Thirty-seven people left Knox on a bus,
In clothing with nary a muss.
They toured the neat city of D.C.,
Seeing all that there was to see,
Then arrived home without any fuss.

There once was an announcer named Ed
Who listened to all that we said.
He walked many miles,
And shared many smiles.
Then fell exhausted into his bed.

There once was a driver named Jim,
Who chauffeured people with any a whim.
He drove us past 'stuff',
Until we had enough.
We would have been lost without him!

If Ed plans another bus run,
With no pain, but plenty of sun,
Just give us a call!
We'll give it our all,
For we don't want to miss any fun!

Comfort

&

Encouragement

IN LOVING MEMORY OF ZEUS

*Today we gave our special pet
A gift so fine and rare.
A gift that will last forever.
A gift that told him we care.*

*We helped him enter heaven
To ease his discomfort and pain,
Where angels will watch over him
As they already knew his name.*

*Here on earth, a part of Zeus
Forever with us will be.
Pictures in albums and our minds,
Each one a precious memory.*

*Enjoying great memories of us,
Zeus is happier now than ever.
Does 'he' or 'we' have any regrets?
Never! Never! No, Never!*

TODAY

*Today I worried
Because I forgot
There is no place
Where God is not.*

LIFE'S SHOWERS

"In every life some rain will fall";
No doubt you'll have your share.
But when rain comes, and you feel blue,
My thoughts are with you there.

When life "rains on your parade",
And plans you've made go sour,
Watch for the rainbow sure to come ~~
Any moment ~~ any hour.

" April showers bring May flowers",
We've heard some people say;
But knowing that I think of you
Might brighten up your day.

"Let a smile be your umbrella".
Have faith in every day.
Facing showers with a happy heart
Chases the clouds away.

"This, too, shall pass" ~~ a promise true.
Believe! And clouds will flee.
New sun will shine upon your life,
And you will happy be.

No need to face alone bad days;
No muddy puddles trod;
Because you can depend on me ~~
Family ~~ friends ~~ and God.

I PRAYED FOR YOU TODAY

Your needs were brought to God today,
While on my knees in prayer.
He saw my tears and heard my pleas,
Then quickly met me there.

We talked; and as I shared with Him
Concerns I have for you,
He listened with a tender heart
Because He loves you, too.

I asked for Him to closely walk
Beside you through this day;
Protecting, healing, cheering you,
And making smooth your way.

Tomorrow when we meet again,
My God will tell me He's
Been helping you along the way
Because He heard my pleas.

Each time I pause and pray for you,
I'm sure He'll meet me there;
For He's a faithful, loving God.
I trust Him for your care.

97

A SEASON OF SUFFERING

*(Definition of 'season': An indefinite period of time
characterized by a particular circumstance.)*

*Just like a bomb, and quick as could be,
Trouble arrived and quickly sent me
Into a season of suffering.*

*I'm thinking back to not long ago,
My life seemed normal, with nary a woe
Before my season of suffering.*

*Sometimes I wonder what's happened to me,
And just how long before I'll be free
From my season of suffering.*

*But I am blessed with a family dear
Who assure me often that they will be near
In my season of suffering.*

*In addition to them, I've friends galore
Who'll assist and aid, and do even more
During my season of suffering.*

*I'm depending on God to give me the strength
To endure, and conquer, whatever the length
Of my season of suffering.*

*When this is behind me, when trouble has flown,
I'll give God the praise, for my faith will have grown
Through my season of suffering.*

MY CONFIDENCE

When my confidence is wavering,
I'll put my trust in God.
He'll lead me and he'll guide me
As on life's path I trod.

He'll give me peace and comfort.
Of my life He'll make more sense.
I know that this is true because
Jesus is my confidence.

DIVINE DIRECTION

Walking through the doors of a church,
I sensed a warmth within my soul.
The smiles and hugs were genuine
And caused my spirit to feel whole.

The music and message spoke to me,
And I knew I need not roam.
God had directed my steps that day
To the Church He knew would be 'home'.

TRUSTING

I'm trusting in Jesus.
He's here by my side.

I'm trusting in Jesus.
He's always my guide.

His timing is perfect.
My hope is in Him.

I'm trusting in Jesus.
In him I abide.

TEARS

When my life is in a muddle
And my tears become a puddle,
With my Jesus I will huddle,

And
I Will
Find
That

Joy comes in the morning.

HOPE

'Hope' is not just a four-letter word
That sometimes is hard to claim;
But it can be found and practiced
If we ask for it in Jesus' name.

SOME TIMES

Some times we smile,
Some times we frown.
Some times we're up,
Some times we're down.

If each new morning
We pause to pray,
We'll feel God's touch
Throughout the day.

GOD'S PRESENCE

I heard God's presence in your voice
As we chatted on the phone.
I know God's presence will stay near,
Even when I feel alone.

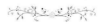

IN MY TIME OF NEED

In my time of need,
God will hear my plea.

In my time of need,
He will come to me.

In my time of need,
I know that I will be

Sheltered in His care.

TO MY CHILD

I trust you, my child.
I trust you to do the right thing.
I trust you to make good choices,
And to yourself honor bring.

Church

Activities / Appreciation

BIBLE SCHOOL DIRECTOR'S PLEA

The date's been set. There's work to be done.
So join the ranks, and join the fun!

Take a card and sign your name,
So that your talent we can claim.

Your help's more precious than a jewel
When put to use in our Bible School.

From Kindergarten to Jr. High,
You'll find a job if you just try.

Or maybe cookies you could provide
Just don't think that you can hide!

We'll need the help of one and all.
Please answer 'yes' when on you we call.

A big success this School can be
If cooperation comes from you and me.

Some time today, the cards are due.
So, please, can we depend on you?

FATHER OF THE YEAR

With this small gift, it does appear
You've been named "Father of the Year".

"Why me?" you may be wondering.
And so some facts we gladly bring.

Because you always wear a smile
And gladly go the 'second mile'.

Because you've been a faithful painter
Spring and Summer, Fall and Winter.

Because your example encourages many
To use their talents and tithe every penny.

Because your children you did teach
To share God's love, and others reach.

Because you've lived a life that's true,
This honor is bestowed on you.

SUNDAY SCHOOL SUPERINTENDENT

The past year is gone,
But memories still linger.
So let's pause for a moment
And count on each finger.

We'll recall some things
You've accomplished so far,
And find out for sure
If you're up to par.

We're reasonably sure
You've been on the run;
For you've gained no weight.
So that's number ONE!

The problems with your husband
Number quite a few;
But you've managed 'him' well.
So that's number TWO!

You've guided the Sunday School
And helped it to be
The best in the District.
So that's number THREE!

You've tithed, you've witnessed,
And given far more
Than the law does require.
So that's number FOUR!

We're pleased to report
That you did arrive
On time every Sunday.
So that's number FIVE!

The things you've accomplished
Have all been just grand;
And speaking for others,
You deserve a good hand.

But a rose is what we offer
As a symbol of the year
You've given to the Sunday School
And the people you hold so dear.

So tickle your nose with this red rose,
And enjoy its fragrance so sweet.
Maybe next year you'll have the chance
To take history and make it repeat!

REV. RAY WILSON & FAMILY
(Tune: There's Within My Heart a Melody)

There's within our church a family.
'Wilson' is the name, it seems.
Recently he came to lead us here.
'Breaking records' is his theme.

Preaching, praying, calling,
Are things they love the most.
Keeps them very, very busy,
While they serve us at this post.

REV. WILLIAM MUIR & FAMILY
(Tune: Give of Your Best to the Master)

When Pastor Muir and his wife came,
Two children they brought along.
Then soon God sent little 'Scottie',
And filled their hearts with song.

Soon Pastor Muir was out calling,
Riding his bike here and there.
All the 'Scotch' sermons he brought us
Came after much time in prayer.

While here, he guided the building
Of a parsonage that wasn't too small.
And many hours he spent helping
To build the Fellowship Hall.

SUNDAY SCHOOL ROUND-UP
(Tune: Home on the Range)

Oh, give us a child,
Whether meek or wild,
Even teens or adults will do.
For our Sunday School hopes
Without lassos or ropes,
To fill every available pew.

Chorus:
Help round them up,
And fill our church school corral.
Whether rich or poor,
Jesus' love is still for
Each and every cowboy and gal.

Faith

LIFE'S 'GRAB BAG'

Life is like a 'grab bag' gift.
We never know what we'll get.
But if we trust God to help us each day,
We'll always be happy and have no regret.

MY HEART'S SONG

I used to sing because I was happy,
Especially when my day went well.
In faith, I now make a 'choice' to sing
Songs that cause my heart to swell.

HAND IN HAND WITH JESUS

If daily I walk hand in hand
With Jesus who loves me so much,
I'll always have a peaceful heart
That comes from His personal touch.

NOTHING CAN SHAKE ME!

Nothing can shake me!
God's right by my side.
He welcomes me daily
With His arms open wide.

Then He holds me close,
Drying the tears I've cried.
I am sheltered and safe
As in His arms I abide.

CLOSER TO JESUS

I'm just a little closer
To Jesus tonight.
The heavens seem nearer;
The stars shine so bright.
Yes, I've drawn a little closer
To Jesus tonight.

LIFE'S PROBLEMS

When life's problems don't go away,
Bring fear and depression every day,
If we walk with Jesus mile after mile
Today and tomorrow we'll walk with a smile.

FAITH

I believe my prayers
Are being heard.

I believe my God
Will see me through.

He knows my need,
And He'll under gird.

He'll give me strength
And sustain me, too.

TOTAL TRUST

My soul, body, and the hairs on my head
Are held in God's hands every day.
With that knowledge, and my daily prayers,
I totally trust Him ~~ come what may.

FELLOWSHIP WITH GOD

God's presence is closer than breathing,
And nearer than my hands and feet.
He patiently waits for my response,
So our fellowship can be complete.

DOING GOD'S WILL

If I do the will of God
From the heart of love He gave me,
The world will be a better place
Because I've served Him humbly.

HUNGRY FOR HOPE

When I am hungry for hope
Because dark seems my way,
I quickly call out to my God
Who faithfully shows me the way.

GLADNESS OF HEART

With gladness of heart,
I approach God each day.
By faith, I know He's listening
To every word I pray.

MY TROUBLED WORLD

In the midst of my troubled world,
Christ will still be my hope.
I know great strength He'll give me
That will enable me to cope.

LOSS OR GAIN

Transition's not always easy,
And change often causes some pain;
But as time passes, and we look back,
We discover no loss ~~ just gain.

IMPERFECT LIFE

When life doesn't fall into perfect order,
And has given me an unwanted shove,
I know I'm safe in the arms of Jesus,
For to Him I'm important and loved.

A TALK WITH JESUS

If I will pause to talk with Jesus
Several times throughout the day,
He'll lead me and He'll guide me,
Making sure I know the way.

WHY WORRY?

Today I worried,
Because I forgot
There is no place
Where God is not.

FROM WORRY TO WONDER

When life and its problems assail me,
I ask God to put them asunder.
I trust ~ He does ~ and I marvel ~
My worries have all changed to wonder.

A FAITHFUL GUIDE

God is stronger than any storm
That life can send my way.
If only I place my trust in Him,
He'll faithfully guide each day.

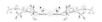

STRESS

With my hurts and heartaches,
I approach God's throne.
He gently mends my spirit,
And assures me I'm not alone.

TRIALS AND BURDENS

Today when I feel overwhelmed,
And heavy laden my heart seems to be,
God's gentle spirit will heed my prayer
And eliminate my anxiety.

A BIG GOD

I'm glad my God is much too big
To fit neatly in my head;
'Cause when my love for him overflows,
I know He's filled my heart instead.

NEW HOPE

When life presents struggles,
And it's hard for me to cope,
My prayers toward heaven
Always fill me with new hope.

HOPE RENEWED

As I trudge along life's rocky path,
Unable to cure the pains of living,
I'll depend on Jesus to give me strength.
Each day new hope He will be giving.

ASSURANCE

Prayer isn't just a place where I 'go'.
It's something I can frequently 'do'.
During these times, God closely listens,
Then assures He cares ~ for me and for you.

LIVE VICTORIOUSLY

Forgetting the 'sweet bye and bye'.
The Bible will teach me how
To live victoriously each day
In the 'nasty now and now'.

NEVER DOUBT GOD'S ABILITY

May I never doubt God's ability
To hear my fervent prayer.
May I ever remember He's waiting,
And eager to meet me there.

PRAYER MAKES A DIFFERENCE

My prayers make a difference
In ways only God knows.
I believe God faithfully listens,
And His mercy on others bestows.

SAFE WITH THE LORD

The Lord watches over me daily,
Protecting from all kinds of harm.
Both my 'comings' and my 'goings'
Are safe from all alarm.

COMINGS AND GOINGS

Trouble and distress will come,
No matter how long I live.
But never will they dash my hopes,
For each problem to Jesus I'll give.

GOD, MY DAILY GUIDE

Though I feel lonely and depressed,
I know God loves me still.
He promises to daily guide me,
If daily I seek His will.

GOD'S UNFAILING LOVE

*May God's unfailing love surround
My life wherever I go.
It's daily walking in His freedom
That gives my life a glow.*

A MOMENT WITH GOD

*God has promised to provide
Sufficient strength for each task;
How soon it comes depends on me,
And when I pause to pray and ask.*

TRUST IN GOD

*This day is the Lord's,
And also the night.
Therefore, I'll trust Him
To do what is right.*

GOD'S BLESSINGS

When I focus on the present,
Taking time to look around,
I'm amazed and ever thankful
For God's blessings that abound.

BLESSED ABUNDANTLY

It only takes a moment
To look around and see
God's love in many places.
I've been blessed abundantly!

PRAYER FOR CHILDREN

While praying for my children,
I asked for their protection;
And then for God to guide them
With His divine direction.

RUN TO MEET JESUS

Whatever my discouragement,
Facing danger, or feeling despair,
I can always run to seek Jesus.
He's promised He'll meet me there.

PATIENCE

When trials come,
One thing's for sure ~
They'll soon be history
If I patiently endure.

SATAN'S DARTS

When Satan's darts of dim dismay
Cross my path, causing disarray,
I'll quickly pause and quietly pray
For God to strengthen me each day.

YES, IT'S ENOUGH

It's enough to know how much God truly loves me.
It's enough to be assured I'm in his care.
It's enough to feel His tender arms around me.
It's enough to sense He hears my whispered prayer.

GOD IS WAITING

In the cold, cold chill
Of my human despair,
I cried out to God ~
He was waiting there.

VISITING THE ILL

If going to visit someone who's ill
And in need of someone to care,
Speak with Jesus before you go.
He'll give you the words to share.

SPEAK KINDLY

If what I say and what I do
Builds walls or bridges between me and you,
Then we must always do and say
The kindest thing, in a pleasant way.

I'M RICH

My earthly inheritance will be small
When with 'God's gift' it's compared.
Eternity will show that I am rich ~
Because of what God has prepared.

CHANGES

Though changes seem to unsettle,
And sometimes bring us pain,
With God's help, we'll overcome
And experience untold gain.

MY CONSCIENCE

The quiet voice of my conscience
Faithfully speaks softly to me.
My conduct will then speak loudly
Of the person God helps me to be.

DISCIPLINE & GRACE

Today, though I struggle,
There's one thing I know:
God's discipline and His grace
Are blessings that help me grow.

WISDOM AND WORDS

During this day, Lord, as you need me
To encourage someone whom you love,
Please bless me with wisdom and words ~
Plus your special strength from above.

THE WAYS OF THE LORD

The ways of the Lord are perfect,
And continuously prompt me to be
An example of His love and grace ~
The person he needs the world to see.

GOD IS THINKING OF ME

It's a splendid thing to realize
God's constantly thinking of me.
He keeps a gentle ear turned my way,
Just waiting to hear my earnest plea.

OPTIMISM

Optimism is important,
And plays a vital role
By helping us look forward
As we strive to reach a goal.

TROUBLES COME AND GO

When troubles come,
I always know
I can depend
On them to go!

STRENTH FOR EACH DAY

When I find I'm weak as a feather,
And my energies have all gone away,
I'll relax in the arms of Jesus ~
The one who gives strength for each day.

SMALL ENCOURAGEMENTS

Small encouragements come into my life.
Sometimes daily they arrive and bring cheer.
Whatever the form, I know they're from God.
It's His way of reminding me He's near.

WHEN I FEEL DISMAY

God can mend the fracture of my heart
And my spirit, when I feel dismay.
By faith I'll trust Him, for I know
He'll lead me to a better day.

THE STRENGTH OF MY HEART

My flesh and my health may fail.
My treasures may also depart;
But life with Jesus will still give joy,
For He is the strength of my heart.

DAY BY DAY

Day by Day
And test by test,
God will provide
Perfect peace and rest.

THE QUIET HEART

It is the quietness of my heart
In the midst of trouble and strife,
That allows God's grace to work in me
Restoring peace and calm in my life.

JESUS IS MY GUIDE

If I will pause to talk with Jesus
Several times throughout the day,
He'll lead me and He'll guide me ~
Making sure I know the way.

LIFE'S DEMANDS

Every demand that's
Part of my day
Is a demand upon God,
If I take time to pray.

SOMEONE PRAYED FOR ME

When changes come into my life
And the future I can't foresee,
That's when I'll pause to remember,
Someone promised to pray for me.

WHAT'S IMPORTANT TO GOD?

It's not what I 'get'
As through life I trod;
It's what I 'become'
That's important to God.

LOOK TO THE PSALMS

When I feel stressed
And in need of some calm,
Quite often the answer
Can be found in a Psalm.

A REMINDER FROM GOD

When trials and burdens are heavy,
And my first thought is to flee,
God quiets my inner being
With the reminder He cares for me.

GOD'S LOVE FLOWS

By day, the Lord gives me a touch.
At night, His song is with me.
His presence gives me daily strength,
As his love flows so full and free.

DELIGHTING IN GOD

God gives me joy.
In Him I delight.
Daily he lifts me
To a brand new height.

COMFORT OF GOD'S SON

Life doesn't always seem fair,
And definitely not always fun.
That's when I pause, take time to pray,
And find I'm comforted by God's Son.

SHARING LOVE

Each man's life is but a breath
Away from God's tomorrow.
So today I'll do my very best
By sharing love ~ not sorrow.

KNOW GOD'S PEACE

No God, no peace.
It's true for you and me.
Know God, Know peace,
Living life full and free.

IN STEP WITH GOD

The very steps we take,
Directed by our God,
Will lead, guide, and keep us
As through life's path we trod.

THE LIFE WE LIVE

The life we live
Is preparation for
The eternity we'll face
Forever and ever more.

WE'VE COME TO MEET YOU, LORD

We've come to meet you here, oh Lord.
We've come to meet you here.
We bring our hearts, our lives, our souls
We've come to meet you here.

I WANT TO BE A GIVER

I want to be a giver,
And give Christ all I've got.
I want to be a giver,
And give to others a lot.

I want to let Christ show
In my life each day.
And tell other people
About the Christian way.

MY GUIDE

Someone is keeping an eye on me
As over life's path I trod.
Someone is keeping an eye on me.
And that Someone is God.

He guides my life each day,
As I go along my way.
I'm thankful that I can say ~
Someone is keeping an eye on me.

WONDROUS LOVE

The Lord works in such wondrous ways
And brightens all my dreary days.
For when I'm feeling very sad,
He lingers close; and makes me glad
That I am sheltered in His care.
Then happiness becomes my fare.

For I have learned through trials o'er
That if I trust Him evermore,
Each day with me He will abide;
And in His arms I'm free to hide.
For all the burdens of this world,
His grace to me has been unfurled.

The next time you are feeling blue,
Here's what I wish that you would do:
Just kneel right down upon your knees
And call to God. He'll hear your pleas.
Very soon your burdens will rise
To be cared for up in the skies.

God's just waiting for your prayer.
To raise you from earth's ugly snare;
To brighten all your living hours
With His loving wondrous powers.
How thankful we should ever be
He loves unknowns ~ like you and me.

A PRAYER FOR TODAY

Strength for today
Is all I ask
From Thee, dear Lord;
To do each task;
To love all others
As You love me.
Just strength for today
I ask of Thee.

GOD'S GOODNESS

God is always so good to us,
Directing our lives through the years.
Our faith will grow throughout that time
As He brings joy that cancels out tears.

BUILDING FAITH

With God looking over my shoulder,
And Christ Himself as my judge,
I'll depend on them completely;
So my faith will not wither or budge.

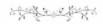

140

MY PROBLEM

Dear Lord, I have a problem.
It seems too great for me.
It's thrown me into darkness
'Til daylight I can't see.

I cannot tell my dearest friends
On earth, you realize;
For they might run and tell another.
Guess you've heard how gossip flies!

It can't be told to all the world;
They wouldn't understand.
Today, then, I'll call on you
And leave it in your hand.

Surely I must bother you
More than most any one.
I bet you're tired of hearing my
Pleas, when day is done.

I've always trusted you before
In matters such as this,
Knowing your grace on me would fall,
My doubts and fears dismiss.

So today I'm here to call on You
This one more time, it seems.
I'll leave the matter at your feet
To be cleansed in heaven's streams.

Dear Lord, I have a problem.
It's much too great for me.
Please help me out of darkness
So daylight I can see.

MY FRIEND

Dear Lord, I'm a little new
At calling on your name;
But praying's become my practice
Since to Your throne I came.

For years I'd been unsettled,
Unhappy, afraid, alone.
And all life's 'little things'
Brought anger to my tone.

But then a sweet and lovely
Friend from out my past ~
Instructed me so that on You
My burdens I could cast.

The friend of mine has known You
For many, many years.
Not once have you forsaken her;
But always calmed her fears.

Because of You, my heart is free,
And all my cares have flown.
Others know I'm happy, for
I'm singing in a sweeter tone.

Yes, I'm going to try her way
And see if I can have
The strength that she possesses,
That soothes her like a salve.

I'm hoping soon that I can boast
A smile just like my friend.
Then we'll both be happy,
Clear to the other end!

PRAYER

While on my knees in prayer today,
I gave God all my fears;
My yesterdays, tomorrows, too;
Because I know he cares.

He felt my anguish, heard my cry
As prayers to Him were winging.
Soon my heart was filled with joy!
He set my soul to singing.

LOVING OTHERS

Having love for one another
Is really quite easy to do.
With Jesus' love within my heart,
It can travel from me to you.

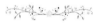

HOME

Whether the home you now live in
Is old, or 'brand-spanking' new,
May the light of God's presence be near
Bringing joy and happiness to you!

MY WALK WITH JESUS

Hand in hand with Jesus
I've walked for many years;
Through times of joy and laughter,
Sometimes sorrow. Sometimes tears.

Encouraging, writing, praying,
I've faithfully 'run the race',
Touching the lives of others,
As I held God's hand of grace.

Sharing the love God gave me
Always brings joy to my heart.
I've seen lives that were changed forever
When God used me for that part.

My 'older lady' future has started.
I know I'll find it grand.
I will walk with Jesus always
As I hold my Master's hand.

A BLESSING IN DISGUISE

While living in a neighborhood,
Quite often I would find
Trash thrown in our yard ~
Every description, every kind.

At first it really upset me.
The nerve of those passing by!
And then one day God nudged me.
"Here's something that's worth a try."

"As you stoop to pick up each piece
Of trash that's been thrown your way,
Quickly pray for that person,
And I will bless them that day."

No longer did I dread that chore!
It was a privilege God gave me.
I counted it a 'double blessing'
And the yard from trash was free.

I BELIEVE

I believe in the one
No eye can see.
I believe in the one
Who created me.

SHARING

As my life on earth grows shorter,
I'm getting my 'ducks in a row'.
By sharing my faith with others,
To heaven they also might go.

Other Writings

TEARS IN THE NIGHT

Sleepless nights. Frustrating days. Tissues in abundance. As I lost considerable vision in my right eye, then just six months later lost similar vision in the left eye, the above-mentioned trials entered my life.

Walking along the shaded lane beside the river where God had planted my husband and me just two years earlier, I spent a lot of time with this routine: walk, cry, walk, sing, walk, cry, walk, pray. Because I could no longer drive, continue with the job I enjoyed, and had to forfeit the computer responsibilities at my church, there was an abundance of time to do the walking-crying-walking-singing-walking-crying-walking-praying ritual.

And then night would fall. Somehow, it always seems that problems are magnified at nightfall. My 'tears in the night' were interspersed with mere dozing, and hugs from my loving husband.

Being a woman of faith, I called upon my Pastor to anoint me, (which is Biblical), and the congregation joined the prayer by laying their hands on me. Time would reveal that healing of my vision was not in God's plan.

As days turned to weeks, I realized my routine was changing. My strolling along the lane by the river included <u>just</u> walking, singing, and praying. In a month's time, God had brought me through my tearful journey ~ ~ and graced me with His wonderful peace. What a perfect healing God had planned for me!

That awesome peace elicited a new prayer: How was God going to use the 'new me'?

Mother Theresa was once asked what her first words to God would be when she arrived in heaven. Her answer brings chuckles to my soul even after several years: "What in the world were you thinking?!"

Like her, I don't claim to understand God's 'thinking'. However, I've learned to accept, and to trust His perfect plan for my imperfect life. Through the process of changes in my life, I've learned to trust. My faith has grown to the point that I no longer feel the need to understand the 'whys'.

For myself personally, I don't believe God 'zapped' me with macular degeneration and significant loss of vision. I know without a doubt, however, that he was aware of the fact that I would be pronounced legally blind. Could He have changed the course of the disease and freed me from my 'new' life and its

150

limitations? Absolutely! Did He choose, however, to keep His hands off, and permit me to continue experiencing what I have? Absolutely on that one, too!

His reasoning? I believe He knew the potential of bringing glory to Himself; for that's the purpose for our creation ~ ~ to bring glory and honor unto Him.

In the past few years, there have been countless opportunities for me to testify to the goodness of God and His blessing on my personal life ~ ~ times of witnessing that I never expected to be afforded to me.

One of the greatest tools He has used through me was the publication of a small book titled "A Treasury of Inspiring Thoughts". Hundreds of people I will never meet have been touched, allowing His word to penetrate their thinking. Wow!

Through the marvel of computers and their magnifying capabilities, two new ministries have become a part of my life. First, a weekly letter goes out to shut-ins. The whimsical, cute, or beautiful stationery brightens the start of their week with humor, my daily 'comings and goings', animal and nature stories from around our country home, etc.

A second ministry is a 20-week (one letter weekly) encouragement series that is shared with people going through extremely difficult times and circumstances.

What a blessed person I am! Is it fun managing daily with such limited vision? No! God, however, has blessed me with family members and friends who lend a hand and enable me to accomplish some of my dreams.

I have learned that the peace that Jesus gives is worth far more than vision – or anything else. And there's a bonus! God has been using me for His purpose, for His glory, and all in His time. There is nothing I want more than His perfect peace. I remain thankful, awed, and amazed at His power and His personal touch on my life.

Today, if I was forced to 'choose' between eyesight and peace, I would definitely choose the latter. Is it an inconvenience being legally blind? Yes. Is it sometimes a nuisance? Yes. Does it place a greater burden on others who are helping bear the load of my needs and requests? Yes. But I know, I know, I know that God is in it. I am a privileged and loved child of His. I am happy, content, and willing to continue being His servant.

My faith is stronger than ever before, and I know

people are watching me.   They're not watching to see <u>how</u> I manage.   They're watching to see <u>why</u> I am so happy and content.

Tears in the night.   Sometimes they still flow ~ ~ but for a different reason.   In the quiet and darkness, my heart overflows with thankfulness that God has chosen to use me as His servant. My tears in the night have now become tears of joy!

THINGS I HAVE LEARNED

1. I've learned that human relationships fare better when we build bridges, instead of walls.

2. I've learned that being an optimist or a pessimist is a personal choice, and that optimists are the happier of the two.

3. I've learned that people change for the better when they are loved unconditionally.

4. I've learned that using the word 'possibly' instead of 'probably' in conversation helps to curb a presumptuous attitude.

5. I've learned to focus on people's good qualities instead of their bad ones.

6. I've learned that love enables people to do the impossible.

7. I've learned that with God's help, old hurts lose their power to twist the way I view people.

8. I've learned the secret to contentment is to let God have complete control of my life.

9. *I've learned that if I let God do the judging and changing of people, all that's left for me to do is love.*

10. *I've learned that love always wins ~ maybe not instantly, but eventually.*

11. *I've learned that walking away from an argument doesn't mean I've lost.*

12. *I've learned that God uses people to do His work.*

13. *I've learned that no one has ever died because they smiled too much.*

14. *I've learned to daily accept the things I cannot change.*

15. *I've learned that God will bless me for the angry words I do not speak.*

16. *I've learned that during a conversation, the "tone" of my voice is more important than the message I'm conveying.*

17. *I have learned that the peace Jesus gives is worth far more than anything else.*

WHEN PARENTS AGE

Watching a parent become more frail and less able to handle their life is not easy to watch or to deal with. From experience, I know it's easy to become frustrated with their memory losses, with their lessened desire to be active, with their constant chatter about their ailments, with their shortened tempers, and with their changing personalities.

I've learned that they can't help but be the new person they're becoming. I've also learned that this is the time in their life when we need to love them abundantly ~ ' in spite of'.

I've learned it's not our responsibility to change them back into the person they once were. It is our responsibility, though, to always react with acceptance, patience, and kindness.

I've learned that when they become obnoxious, it's the time to 'show' love ~ even when we might not 'feel' love at the moment. Love enables us to do the impossible.

I've learned we can raise our tolerance level by lowering our expectations of the older person.

I've learned it's very important for them to continue making decisions and choices ~ even though the decision might shorten their life ~ even though we might not be in agreement. It's still their life; and we should respect their right to make even 'wrong' choices.

I've learned that the 'tone' of our voice is sometimes more important than the 'message' we're conveying. If we can put our strong feelings about a particular issue aside, choose our words carefully, then present the idea with love and calmness, quite often matters or disagreements can be resolved pleasantly for everyone involved.

I've learned that providing for an elderly person's emotional happiness is sometimes more important than providing for their physical welfare. Eliminating some of the activities and foods that the older person once enjoyed might provide a longer life - - but sometimes living an hour, a day, or a week longer is just not 'worth it' to the aging person. They need those moments of joy!

I've learned it's not our job to scold if the older person expresses a lack of desire to live much longer. They need to have the liberty of expressing their true feelings ~ without the fear of being reprimanded.

I've learned that some of the adverse changes in their lives are possibly part of God's plan ~ as He allows the things of this world to become less appealing. Maybe He sometimes allows nature to take its downward course, making it easier for the older person to leave this earth. When strength is gone, death becomes more desirable than life. I've learned we're not responsible for the aging person's 'action' - - but we are responsible for our 'reaction'. If our reactions are based on love and respect, we will have no regrets to live with after our parents are gone.

I've learned the respect shown the elderly, along with the love, the time, the energy and the patience invested, is never in vain.

I've learned that God will bless us for the angry words we do not speak when we are totally frustrated and utterly exhausted. During our most agonizing moments, it's helpful to pause and think: "What would Jesus do right now for this person if He were here? How would Jesus show love in this situation? What would be the response of Jesus to this elderly and hurting person? " This kind of thinking often provides the necessary perspective when our tolerance has reached a low point, or when decisions are needing to be made.

Finally, I've learned we can depend on God to lead and guide us along the way - - if our motives toward the elderly are pure. We, and our aging parents, are loved unconditionally by our Heavenly Father. He will provide the physical and emotional strengths we need as we face each day. He is faithful!

WHEN GOD DOES (Or Does Not) CHOOSE TO HEAL

The year was 1946, and I had just completed first grade. It seemed to me that I was spending way too much time in the doctor's office. A persistent fever was the reason for the doctor visits. If I had thought the doctor's office visits were bad, a full week in the hospital for testing was obnoxious. Without the aid of X-rays available yet in the medical field, a fluoroscope revealed a fungus growing in both my lungs. The verdict? The doctors prescribed complete bed rest for six months. What I know now, but didn't know then, was that my parents were told I would be dead before the 6-month period ended.

BUT, I remember the day some of the church people arrived at our home to pray. I was carried to the living room, where they knelt around me, and fervently asked God to heal me. At the end of only three months, God had completed the healing process. With the doctor's blessing, I remember running out to the back yard where a swinging trapeze was waiting for me. With a run and a jump, I quickly was swinging upside-down by my heels!

God's purpose for my healing? First, I believe it provided a testimony to God's mighty power. Secondly, He had provided a way to use my life ~ for Him. As He supplied me a great husband and four children, plus an office job that I loved, He found many ways to use the talents He had given me. Talents that provided opportunities within the Church, and also to be an encourager to His people. In my young life, he knew I would be a willing and useful tool to do His work.

During a routine eye exam in my late 40's, I was diagnosed with Macular Degeneration. Usually, that is an eye disease that doesn't raise it's ugly head until much later in life. Thankfully, it didn't lessen my vision until my early 60's. Suddenly, blood vessels in both eyes began to hemorrhage. Laser surgeries stopped the bleeding, but vision was lost in the process. In less than a 6-month period of time, many things in life that I had taken for granted stopped. I was pronounced legally blind. For myself, though, I preferred to say I had limited vision. Unable to see anyone's face, conversations were awkward ~ almost like speaking to a telephone pole. Often I needed help when shopping, etc. A business card I could present to someone assisting me seemed to be a good answer:

> *It's plain to see that I can't see*
> *Nearly as well as you can.*
> *So if you'll help me, I'll gladly thank thee.*
> *Now don't you think that's a good plan?*

Activities I had enjoyed for years came to a screeching halt ~ volunteer church activities, a job in the business world, driving and going anywhere by myself. What to do? Immediately I remembered the healing God gave

*me at the age of seven. Contacting my Pastor, an
anointing along with the prayers of my church family,
was provided.*

*God, however, had other plans. This time, He chose not
to heal. Why? At some point, He reminded me of the
writing talents I was born with ~ thanks to Him! Thus,
my writing ministry of encouraging letters to those
traveling a tough road became my "Joy in the Mailbox"
ministry. God provided me with stationery, stamps and
the names of people who needed a special touch. Once
again, it was God using me to do His work.*

*Ten years passed, and my life seemed to be on an even
keel. Recently, however, I've found myself living among
the old folks. Occasionally, I was even brave enough to
verbally acknowledge that I was an old lady. Actually, it
hasn't seemed to be an extremely emotional time in my
life.*

*Until ~ yes, the 'until' has a new meaning for me.
Noticing my strength and energy had waned, and that
my body was suffering multitudinous aches, pains and
other weird sensations, I consulted my doctor for an
answer. I don't really care for the diagnosis I received.
Lupus. What a simple name for a complicated disease.
In my heart, I knew immediately it was time to exercise
my faith.*

*In a Sunday morning service, the Pastor once again
called the congregation to prayer. The touch of the*

anointing oil reminded me of God's presence in my life. My faith soared! Not because I knew He would heal me, but because I know He knows my name. He knows the plans He has for me. And, yes, He knows the possible ways He can continue to use me for His glory.

For that reason, I don't feel the need to ask Him why he sometimes does heal; and other times He doesn't. He, and only He, can choose the perfect path for a life He has created. He, and only He, knows I am comfortable in His care. He also knows I'm willing to continue as His servant, as He may choose to use me in His work.

ABOUT THE AUTHOR

As a child, Maurine (Wolters) Wilder discovered the joy of connecting words that rhymed. When a 6th grade teacher required each student to write a poem, Maurine took pencil in hand, grabbed a piece of paper, and she was 'off and running'!

More than 60 years later, numerous poems and writings continue to bring joy into her life.

Throughout her life she has used her rhyming / writing talent to encourage and cheer family and friends.

With the blessing of husband Josh and her four children (Daryl, Daryn, Annette, Lynette), Maurine's collection of poems and writings have herewith been compiled.

Her passion of encouraging, cheering and uplifting others is exemplified in words from her heart.
Born in Columbus, Indiana, she grew up in Phoenix, Arizona. After marriage, she moved to Winamac, Indiana where she and her husband still reside.

Maurine is a person of faith, and firmly believes that God often uses people to do His work. She is hopeful the words in this book will enhance, inspire, and bring laughter into the lives of others.